Sandhurst

in old picture postcards

by
Kitty Dancy OBE
and
Allan Brooker

European Library – Zaltbommel/Netherlands

Cover picture:
Mr. Thomas Mills of Longdown Lodge had made his fortune in the Australian goldfields, and returned to England to enjoy the life of an English Country Gentleman. (Mrs. K. Dancy.)

GB   ISBN 90 288 5361 8 / CIP

© 1992 European Library – Zaltbommel/Netherlands

INTRODUCTION

Sandhurst is a name of Saxon origin; Sand — referring to the type of soil, and — hurst — a wooded eminence. Sandhurst is situated on the border of Berkshire, separated from Hampshire by the River Blackwater, and from Surrey by the Wish Stream, which flows through the grounds of the Royal Military College founded for the training of officers of the British Army in 1812 and which gives Sandhurst its claim to fame.

The census figures at the time of the Enclosure Acts of 1805-1817, showed 36 houses and a population of 222; the village boundaries have varied over the years, but for most of the time have reached the borders of Finchampstead, Easthampstead and Wokingham; the most fundamental change was in 1894 when Crowthorne became a separate Parish following the Act of Parliament which established secular Parish Councils. Prior to that date Broadmoor Hospital and Wellington College as well as the Royal Military College had been the three large establishments in Sandhurst that provided local employment. Broadmoor and Wellington College were now within the boundary of the new Crowthorne.

Sandhurst is not mentioned in the Doomsday Book; the first record is found in the Exchequer Rolls of the 21st year of Henry II (1175) when the receipt of one mark for the 'Villata de Sandhurst' is recorded. In 1222 there is evidence of a chapel in Sandhurst on the site of the present St. Michael's Church. Very little is known of the early history, of this area which was in the territory of the Attribates, which is remembered in the Roman name for Silchester, 'Calleva Attrebatum' and the link with the Roman military road joining Londinium (London) with Pontes (Staines) and Calleva Attribatum (Silchester) known locally as the Devil's Highway, with the high point known as Ceasar's Camp, just north of the built up area of Sandhurst.

Windsor Forest enclosed this area, and the last keeper of Sandhurst Walk was Major General Cox who died in 1788, and is buried in Sandhurst churchyard. Everyone living within the area was subject to Forest laws, which were designed for the preservation of game and deer. The human inhabitants took second place; poaching was punished with utmost severity right up to the 19th century. Freeholders had the right to pasture sheep and cattle on the waste of the forest and to collect 'brouse wood' and rootage. Land referred to as Poors Land on the Enclosure maps of 1816 was lost to local people and much hardship was caused to the community at the loss of ancient grazing and other rights. One protest song ran:

> *They hang the man and flog the woman*
> *That steal the goose from off the common*
> *But let the greater villain loose*
> *Who steals the common from the goose*

1848 saw the construction of the South Eastern and Chatham railway line, known affectionately as the Slow, Easy and Comfortable; the itinerant work force needed accommodation locally and the area behind the New Inn became known as Babylon; perhaps because of the behaviour of the men living there! The large house known as Rivermead was converted to the Railway Tavern.

Many large houses, gardens and farms were developed in the late 1800's. Girls went into domestic service and men worked in the gardens, stables and farms. Sandhurst Lodge – the local Manor House – at one time employed 17 gardeners, and had a lake, heated by gas to enable exotic plants to be grown. Those large houses that remain, have been converted into flats. The gardens have housing estates covering them, the farms have gone and farm animals have been replaced by the motor car. By-pass roads have been constructed to enable people to travel to work miles away and to bring people into the vast car parking facilities, for 2,000 cars, provided by Marks and Spencer and Tesco Superstores at The Meadows!

There are still the open spaces of Edgebarrow Woods, Snaprails, and Ambarrow Court, and also a walk across the Memorial Fields to the River Blackwater to remind one of rural Sandhurst of days gone by.

After the Second World War, the Royal Military College and Royal Artillery Woolwich, amalgamated and became The Royal Military Academy. In 1974 Sandhurst became a Town and in 1991 there is a population of about 20,000.

The lay-out of this book is as follows: first Royal Military College, then College Town, on to Central Sandhurst, then under the railway bridge to Little Sandhurst.

Acknowledgements:
We, the compilers, would like to thank all the people who offered pictures and views of Sandhurst plus the knowledge and memories without which the book could not have been completed. Special thanks go to Colin Sinnott for the use of so many cards from his collection, and also to Maurice Clark and Mr. and Mrs. Stubley.

We would like to thank Mr. Wells of M.J.W. photographs of Chessington, for reproducing all the pictures from the originals to such a high standard.

Acknowledgement and thanks to the University of Reading, 'The History of Sandhurst' book for information, and to Mrs. Sylvia Trevis for the typing.

North Entrance to Sandhurst Military College.

1. North entrance to Sandhurst Military College in 1906; the Gate Keeper's house is situated on the bend in the Yorktown Road, Sandhurst. The Gate Keeper, usually a retired soldier, who resided with his family in the lodge, had the responsibility for opening the gates and monitoring the people passing through. The path to the left led to staff married quarters and to the rear of the main college buildings. The path to the right led past the drive to the Commandant's house, then onto the front of the main college building on the left, and the playing fields and the lake on the right and through to Yorktown and Camberley. (Alan Kane.)

2. View of the Royal Military College taken from the air at Christmas 1920, by a photographer flying in a R.A.F. plane from Farnborough. In the far distance are some of the houses built in what was to become College Road and Branksome Hill Road, and the open heathland of Owlsmoor. (Mr. and Mrs. George Clarke.)

Royal Military College, Camberley

3. The picture states Royal Military College, Camberley, but it is geographically in Sandhurst. This picture, post marked 1908 shows a parade of cadets in front of the Main Building. This parade ground is still used for the cadets Passing Out Parades in 1991, when they qualify to become officers in the British Army. (Mr. C. Sinnott.)

4. The New Building, Royal Military College erected in 1912 prior to the outbreak of War in 1914 when the peace establishment of cadets was 650. (University of Reading.)

5. This picture shows the carriages available at Camberley Railway Station waiting to take Cadets and Staff to the Royal Military College at the beginning of term in 1890. (Mr. Henry Purvey.)

6. A view of the Boat House across the College Lake. Boating was used on many social occasions in the Royal Military College. (Mr. C. Sinnott.)

Royal Military College, Sandhurst. *[...]*

7. The Royal Military College Lake in 1901. This view would have been much appreciated by local people who at that time had freedom of access to enjoy the beautiful scenery, watch the cricket matches and other games, as well as the formality of the Passing Out Parades. (Mr. C. Sinnott).

The Drive and Lake. R.M.C. Sandhurst. B920.

8. The Drive and Lake of the Royal Military College at Sandhurst. This was the route used by local people walking from Sandhurst to Yorktown, or even perhaps biking, as shown by the man in the picture. (Mr. C. Sinnott.)

York Town, Entrance to Sandhurst Military College.

9. The Yorktown Entrance to the Royal Military College in 1906, showing the Gate Keeper's Lodge; this is on the Surrey side of the Wish Stream. (Alan Kane.)

10. The Woods, Royal Military College, 1895. The grounds were a heavily wooded area which was at one time within the boundaries of the Royal Windsor Forest. (Mr. C. Sinnott.)

CHINESE BRIDGE, R.M.C.   SANDHURST.   P. 112

11. The Chinese Bridge in 1910 which went over the Wish Stream separating the Royal Military College from the Staff College; the Staff College was for the training of Senior Army Officers. (Mr. C. Sinnott.)

12. The Chapel R.M.C. in 1901. Consecrated and brought into use in 1879, the design was taken from a church in Florence, Italy. (Mr. C. Sinnott.)

13. The interior of the Royal Military College Chapel in 1901. It was copied from the Cathedral Church in Siena, being a combination of alabaster and choice marbles. (Mr. C. Sinnott.)

Christ Church, Royal Military College, Sandhurst.

14. Christchurch, Royal Military College Chapel in 1921, following the extension and re-designing which was dedicated by the Archbishop of Canterbury on 5th May 1921. The Chapel is a unique shrine to the Officers Corps of the British Army. (Mr. C. Sinnott.)

Christ Church, Royal Military College, Sandhurst.

15. The interior of the R.M.C. Chapel in 1921. Towards the end of the First World War it was proposed that the rebuilding of the Chapel should be a memorial to over 4,000 Sandhurst Cadets. No public funds were available and so the very bricks had to be paid for by private subscription. The names of those Sandhurst Cadets who gave their lives in the Great War are carved into the marble of the pillars and panels of the chancel and nave. (Mr. C. Sinnott.)

Camberley, Royal Military College, Memorial to all men"

16. Memorial to all men. Royal Military College 1927. (Mr. C. Sinnott.)

17. 'The Jolly Farmer', a picture taken from the junction of College Road and Yorktown Road, post marked 11th April 1914. On 5th September 1854 application was made by Benjamin Heath, farmer and beer seller, for a licence for the sale of beer under the sign 'The Jolly Farmer' near the Royal Military College in Sandhurst. It was notified that if granted he would not re-new the licence for the 'canteen' at the college – granted. Being so close to the R.M.C., staff, both civilian and military, could 'slip out' for a 'quick one'. (Mr. C. Sinnott.)

18. College Road Sandhurst. View taken from near the junction with Yorktown Road, postmark 27th June, 1925. (Mr. C. Sinnott.)

19. Canadian Y.M.C.A. Mission Hall in 1917. Built in 1913, pulled down in 1970, it was situated in Branksome Hill Road, which was made as a gravel road in 1900. Canadian lumber-jacks worked in this area during the First World War felling timber and they used a gravity rail system to get the felled timber down to the railway siding. (Mrs. F. Score.)

20. College Town School, Branksome Hill Road in 1920. This school was opened on 2nd September 1907. The Headmaster was Arthur John Pearce who stated in the school log book 'To-day I took charge of new school, upwards of 120 children were entered.' By 1911 he was reporting on the bad state of the roads and seeing the indifferent state of many of the children's boots, 'I am recommending the parents provide clogs for winter months; a firm will supply Lancashire clogs at 2/11 a pair.' (Mrs. F. Score.)

21. The 1908 class from College Town School in Branksome Hill Road. Back row: Sybil Saunders, Maud Compton, Queeny Hammond, ..., Dolly Pierce, Alison Leggett, ... and Mr. Brown. Second row: Mr. Pierce (Headmaster), Albert Dracott, ..., Richard Score, ..., Alfred Seeby, ..., ? Rose, ..., ..., Harold Dracott and Teresa Doran. Third row: ...., Bertha Doors, Florence Young, Ada Webb, Winnie Diskin, Eva Webb, Iris Green, Rene Doran, Elsie Moore, Eleanor Seeby and Marjorie Pierce. Front row: Ronald Saunders, ? Clifford, Freddie Grant, Harold Pierce, ..., Walter Hammond, Reg.Saunders, Harold Cahil, ..., ... (Mrs. F. Score.)

22. Bull and Butcher Pub; meeting of the hunt. (Mr. Henry Purvey.)

23. Old Bull and Butcher Pub. Yorktown Road. Picture taken from a newspaper clipping 1905. (Mr. C. Jones.)

24. Owlsmoor Road 1920. On the right side of this road was the open heath area on which the gypsy huts and caravans collected at certain times of the year, when the travellers were not on their journeys helping with planting and harvesting or on fairgrounds in various parts of the countryside. Now all is changed it is the site of Sandhurst Comprehensive School and vast new housing estates. (Mr. Collins.)

FLOODS IN SANDHURST

25. Floods in Sandhurst at the junction of the Owlsmoor Road and Yorktown Road near the Bull and Butcher Pub. (Mr. Henry Purvey.)

26. Wellington Arms on the corner of Yorktown Road and Wellington Road. In 1891 William Purvey took over as landlord and this picture shows their first cars. First car: Mr. Purvey, Jack, Alan and Harold and Aunt Ada. Second car: Mrs. Purvey, Mr. Dickenson and Mrs. Clarke's brother. (Mr. Henry Purvey.)

27. The bend in the Yorktown Road showing Brind Park Terrace and the Wellington Arms with the sign 'Baker's Fine Ales' displayed. (Mr. & Mrs. Croft.)

1939. Sandhurst St. Sandhurst.

28. This is the corner of Green Lane and Yorktown Road looking towards the bend in the road at the Wellington Arms. The fields on the right hand side of the picture were used to graze cattle from Rackstraws Farm. The corner shop was a grocer's, much used as a sweet shop by local children. (Mr. C. Sinnott.)

29. The Grocer's Stores, Yorktown Road with goods displayed outside and a car which should help to date the picture. It is now the glass centre. (Mr. C. Sinnott.)

30. St. Mary's Church, Wellington Road. A snowy scene of the old St. Mary's, built in the late 1800's and demolished in 1965. (John and Jill Lyford.)

31. Choir at St. Mary's Church (circa 1910). Back row, left to right: Maggie Andrews, Beatie Brown, Ethel Collins, Ada Webb, Mr. Clarke, Eleanor Gregory, ..., ..., Edith Seeby and Flossie Dracup. Middle row: Maisey Duck, Ever Webb, Mrs. Clarke, Reverend Leslie, Mrs. Pierce (the School Master's wife and organist), Jessie Evens and Irene Doran. Front row: Violet Seeby and Ivy Dracup. (Miss. V. Seeby.)

32. Snaprails House, which picture was taken about 1934, situated in Wellington Road. It was the home of Mr. & Mrs. Church who played an active part in the village life; the grounds of the estate were used for fetes, garden parties, and open air performances of 'Mid Summer Night's Dream'. Mr. Church was a supporter in the early days of the foundation of Sandhurst Silver Band and the Working Men's Club. The house has been demolished but the grounds have now become a pleasant park and recreation area. (Mrs. F. Dean.)

33. Snaprails Farm was situated to the left of the stream that flowed from the lake in the grounds of Snaprails. The old farm house is still there but the cows have long gone. There were five Jersey cows kept in the Snaprails Field. They provided milk for all who lived and worked there. (Mrs. C. Piper.)

34. Sandhurst Silver Band — used to be called 'The Sandhurst Brass Band' until they won a competition and were able to have their instruments silvered. This picture was taken in 1912 and the members are named where known. From left to right, back row: Joe Evans, Harry Coombes, George Webb, Albert Dalley, Walter Hodge, Harry Gore, ..., ..., Charlie Pike and Bill Austin. Front row: Joe James, ..., ..., ..., Mr. Bennellick, Fred Bennellick, Albert Johnson and Ernest Jeffries. On ground: Bill Coombs, ... (Mr. B. Attewell.)

Thibet Road, Sandhurst.

35. Slate House and Diana Lodge at the junction of Thibet Road and Wellington Road. (Mr. C. Sinnott.)

36. View of Thibet Road as it wound its way up to the open heath that stretched towards Crowthorne and Broadmoor. The house became the home of Reverend Clayton and his family. He was the Curate of St. Mary's Church. (Mr. C. Sinnott.)

37. St. Helen's House, Wellington Road 1887. This picture was taken from an album of photographs belonging to Colonel Harvey of Ambarrow Court. The house was demolished and St. Helen's Crescent has taken its place. (Mrs. K. Dancy.)

38. This wall is at the top of Wellington Road and was built in 1912 with the gateway entrance to Longdown Lodge which was the home of Mr. and Mrs. Mills. Longdown Lodge is now converted into flats. (Mrs. K. Dancy.)

39. The Corner Stores at the junction of Albion Road and Wellington Road. The shop was run by
Mr. & Mrs. Greenfield for 27 years but is now closed. (Mr. M. Greenfield.)

Wellington Road, Sandhurst.

40. A view of Wellington Road looking down towards St. Mary's Church. (Mr. Sinnott.)

SANDHURST 848

41. Albion Road, postmark 4th August 1920, looking from the junction with Yorktown Road. The houses on the left of the picture are still there in 1991. (Mr. C. Sinnott.)

The Broadway.
Sandhurst.

. 3181 .

42. This picture shows how open the ground was, taken from the junction of Yorktown Road looking north. On the far right is Slate House in Thibet Road; the postmark says 26th June 1914. (Mr. R. Cooper.)

8594. The Ford, Sandhurst.

43. The Ford Swan Lane. This picture also shows the footbridge over the River Blackwater; postmark 16th July 1914. For many years local children played and swam in the river. In 1968 a bridge was built over the River Blackwater to enable the increasing vehicle traffic to have an easier ride and not get stuck in the river when water levels were high. (Mr. C. Sinnott.)

44. Wisemans Farm Swan Lane 1927. Miss Daisy Wiseman is standing at the gate. It was a dairy farm and the two daughters used to deliver milk to houses near by. (Mr. P. Burlton.)

45. Smith's the butcher's, Yorktown Road, later became Talmage's, then Allums, and is now in 1991 The Peking Restaurant. Behind the trees on the left of the picture was Nightingale Farm. The Old Farm House is still in York Way, and Nightingale Gardens, a road on the housing estate, is a reminder of the old farm. (Mr. C. Sinnott.)

Yorktown, Road, Sandhurst.

Bignell, Bros., Woodcote, Reading

46. Yorktown Road in 1904. This shop was on the corner of Newtown Road and later became Mrs. Nash's sweet shop that local children loved, because of the wonderful choice of sweets on offer. (Mr. B. Attewell.)

47. Although this picture is marked Yorktown Sandhurst, it is in fact Newtown Road which doesn't look so very different in 1991; it is still an unmade, rutted road. (University of Reading.)

Sandhurst.

Bignell, Bros., Woodcote, Reading.

48. The junction of Yorktown Road and Newtown Road looking towards the railway bridge. Postmark August 17, 1906. (Mr. and Mrs. Clarke.)

Sandhurst, View from Sandhurst Halt.

49. View from Sandhurst Halt of The New Inn and the junction of Yorktown Road and Crowthorne Road. (Mr. C. Sinnott.)

50. New Inn Hill, Sandhurst, looking down towards the railway. In 1991 this is called Crowthorne Road. (Mr. M. Clark.)

51. Uplands House in 1887. This picture is from the album of Colonel Harvey. The house was built in 1886 and situated on the Crowthorne Road. It is said that the Reverend Henry Parsons, the local Rector, built 'St. Helen's', 'Uplands' and 'The Warren' for his daughters when they got married. Uplands Primary School is situated on what was part of the estate, the rest is now covered by houses, and Uplands House has been demolished. (Mrs. K. Dancy.)

52. Harts Leap House has changed its appearance over the years but this is what it looked like on 11th September 1911. It was built by Mrs. Blakeley and later occupied by Mr. Van Der Byl till 1908 when an Indian Prince and his entourage moved in. He left Harts Leap House at the outbreak of war in 1914. Lt.Colonel Stilwell lived there later, still later it was used as a convalescent home for children from the London Hospitals, then it became a Cheshire home for disabled and now for elderly people who need care. (Alan Kane.)

53. The grandfather of Mr. H. Rogers with his wheelbarrow in Harts Leap Road, then known as The Back Lanes; postmark 28th June 1912. At this time men who were out of work would be employed by Dr. Russell to repair local roads as seen in the picture. (Mr. J. Bryant.)

54. Forest End House, built by Mrs. Blakeley. It was her home being the widow of Capt. T. Blakeley R.A., the inventor of a gun which is depicted on his monument in the churchyard. The house, named Forest End, was reckoned to be situated at the end of Windsor Forest. (Mr. & Mrs. Huddle.)

55. This picture shows the Handley family, who lived at Forest End Cottage. Mr. Robert Handley was the gardener at Forest End House and his son was the groom; other names are Clara Smith nee Handley (daughter), Mrs. Martha Handley nee Early — Mrs. Earley was Jane Cox of Sandhurst. They all emigrated to Canada in 1913. (Mr. & Mrs. Huddle.)

The Old Well, Sandhurst.

A. Biggadike
Series 705.

56. The Old Well (with bucket) on Scotland Hill. The well was donated by Mrs. Blakeley and the wording on the well says: 'This well was erected as a memorial to Harriet Walter Vyvan Connell of Forest End who died August 1874.' (Mr. C. Sinnott.)

57. St. Michael's Club, Scotland Hill in 1887 from Col. Harvey's album. The building of this Club was supported by the wealthy people in the village to provide social activities for people − mostly men − who worked in the locality and it was well used and appreciated until the Club was moved to larger premises in Wellington Road in the 1920's. (Mrs. K. Dancy.)

SANDHURST HALL.

58. Russell Hall, Scotland Hill; postmark 21st July 1905. This hall was provided by Dr. Russell who lived and worked in Sandhurst. He was a strong supporter of the Methodist Church and the Russell Hall was built near the church and used for many years for social activities, but is now used as a warehouse in 1991. (Mr. C. Sinnott.)

59. View of the railway bridge over the main road in Sandhurst; it shows the Red House which has now been demolished. (Mrs. C. Piper.)

60. View of the same railway bridge from the other side; leaving Yorktown Road you are now in the High Street. The lane on the right leads to Breech Farm and a footpath to Swan Lane. (Mr. C. Sinnott.)

61. Sandhurst Halt; postmark 9th August 1927. The view is southward and shows a steam train climbing the gradient out of the Blackwater Valley. (Mrs. Cornish.)

62. The wooden bridge over the railway line between the Sandhurst Halt Station and Little Sandhurst. The connecting footpath provided a shorter walk than going along the main road. The house in the background is Perry Hill. The wooden bridge is now replaced by an iron one. (Mrs. Arnold.)

63. Sandhurst High Street showing the bakery, the mill and butcher's, 1900-1910. The manager of Piggs, Bakers and Grocers was Mr. Mathews who is shown standing outside the shop. (Mr. M. Clark.)

64. Sandhurst High Street with the Post Office on the right, the pub sign of The Dukes Head and in the distance the mill chimney. (Mr. M. Clark.)

New Road, Sandhurst

65. New Road, Sandhurst, climbs up the hill from The High Street. It is still a rutted gravel road in 1991, as it was on 11th August 1916. (Alan Kane.)

66. The Rose and Crown pub prior to 1924 when there were radical alterations. The sign reads 'Simpson & Son Cycle Engineers and Cycles for Hire'. The Rose and Crown is probably the oldest licensed premises in Sandhurst of which a Mrs. Hannah Geale was the owner and vendor in 1742. (Mr. L. Bateman.)

67. The Rose and Crown pub with the local hunt outside. This is a picture of the pub after the extensive alterations in 1924. The car belonged to Mr. A. Payne, the builder, who lived next door. (Mrs. Cornish.)

68. High Street in Sandhurst, as it winds its way towards the Yateley Lane. (Mr. J. Bryant.)

69. Blackwater River looking towards St. Michael's Church in 1913. In the picture is Mr. Roger's mother. It is a rural aspect of the riverside that the Blackwater Conservation Project is trying to retain from Aldershot to Wokingham at the present time in 1991. (Mr. Rogers.)

70. Police and Sandhurst Special Constables in 1915: Back row, left to right: J. Eden, L. Goswell, A. Moss, C. Heard, J. Anderson, W. Webb and W. Austin. Centre row: P.C.T. Collyer, V. Hunt, T. Ledger, J. Samson, W. Snook, A. Bandell, P. Stringfellow, H. Eyre, G. Watts, F. Lark and PC.R. Holloway. Front row: W. Dixon, G. Oldham, M. Goddard, Sgt. F. Salter, Major T. Bunting, T. Ledger (Father of T. Ledger, centre row), W. Kent, H. Hakin and J. Clarke.

Their occupations as recalled in 1979: L. Goswell (Bricklayer), A. Moss (Blacksmith), C. Heard (Cycle shed R.M.A.), J. Anderson (College servant), W. Webb (Sports coach R.M.A.), W. Austin (Gardener-Forest End), V. Hunt (Butcher-next to the Mill), W. Snook (Insurance), A. Bandell (Farm hand), P. Stringfellow (Chaufeur-Snaprails), H. Eyre (Fruit grower), G. Watts (Registrar), G. Oldham (Head Teacher C/E School), M. Goddard (Gardener-Ambarrow), Major Bunting (sub-Division Officer), W. Kent (Baker), H. Hakin (Rectory Farm), J. Clarke (Head Groundsman R.M.A.).

71. St. Michael's School from Colonel Harvey's album, 1887. The school was opened in 1862. Old registers show that children attended from a wide area: Blackwater, Finchampstead, Crowthorne, Broadmoor and Eversley; a long way to walk in all weathers on rutted roads with poor footwear and sometimes none at all. A School Inspector's report in 1868 stated: *Arithmetic − intelligent sound; Writing − excellent; Spelling − very good; Reading − fair; Discipline − perfect; Scripture − a failure in all classes.* A hard judgement for a Church School to have to take! The school with additional sections added over the years is still open in 1991. (Mrs. K. Dancy.)

72. Pupils of St. Michael's School in 1902. Mr. Gregory who had been the master of St. Michael's School for 35 years died and the post was advertised. There were over 270 applications and Mr. Oldham of Hale School was appointed at a salary of £100 per annum and the house and garden. Later an assistant mistress for the infants was appointed at £40 per annum. We have not been able to trace the names of the children in this picture. (Mrs. F. Score.)

ST MICHAELS PARISH CHURCH. SANDHURST PRIOR TO 1853

73. This is a drawing of St. Michael's Parish Church in Sandhurst, prior to 1853 when it was pulled down and the present one erected. There is mention of a Chapel on the site in 1220 and repairs ordered in 1408 and the Chaplain getting into trouble for celebrating a secret marriage at night without the Banns being called or a licence. The Geale Memorial was cast out from the old church but recovered by Mr. Reuben Watts, a former Parish Clerk who dug them up. The Geale Memorial is now affixed to the wall of the South Chapel in the present St. Michael's Church. (Mrs. K. Dancy.)

74. St. Michael's Church, Sandhurst, dated 1906; postmark Sandhurst 1st April 1919. This church was built in 1853 under the direction of Mr. G.E. Street. The first incumbent was in 1222: John of Shirborne (Sherborne) and sometimes the Living was vacant and sometimes shared with Yateley or Frimley. The Living came under the Diocese of Sarum (Salisbury) until 1836 when it became part of the Oxford Diocese. (Mr. C. Sinnott.)

The Rectory, Sandhurst.

75. The Old Rectory in Sandhurst. Reverend Henry Parson, incumbent of the Parish Church from 1852-1878, was a wealthy man who had this large Rectory built on the hill opposite St. Michael's Parish Church. This Rectory was demolished and a much smaller one was built to replace it in 1956. (Mrs. K. Dancy.)

76. Cannon Parsons and his wife. A picture taken from Col. Harvey's album, dated 1887. (Mrs. K. Dancy.)

77. Ambarrow Court, a large mansion built in 1885 near Perry Bridge and owned by Col. and Mrs. Harvey. He was a local magistrate and an important person in the Parish. During the Second World War it was linked with the Royal Aircraft Establishment. It was later abandoned and pulled down. The grounds were acquired by Bracknell District Council in 1985, and it now blends in with the adjacent National Trust Land to make a lovely recreational walking area. (From Col. Harvey's album – Mrs. K. Dancy.)

78. Ambarrow Court Lodge showing the gate and the drive. A picture from Col. Harvey's album, dated 1887. The Lodge lasted a little longer than the house but is now demolished and the area is a car park. (Mrs. K. Dancy.)

79. Ambarrow Court stables from Col. Harvey's album, dated 1887. Mrs. Harvey would be seen going through the village in a two-horse open carriage with a liveried coachman, wearing a top hat and cockade, high boots all stiff and looking straight ahead; the whip, tied with a bow, was an ornament to be drawn delicately across the horse's back. With a companion at her side, Mrs. Harvey known as, 'The First Lady of Sandhurst' would be looking to the left and right for the bob and curtsey of acknowledgement. (Mrs. K. Dancy.)

80. The two gardeners with the roller at Ambarrow Court. From Col. Harvey's album, dated 1887. (Mrs. K. Dancy.)

81. All is safely gathered in. Mounting the hay rick. Picture from Col. Harvey's album, dated 1887. (Mrs. K. Dancy.)

82. Sandhurst Lodge. Richard Heaviside acquired the land and the Manor or Lordship of Sandhurst in 1789 and had the house built. It has changed hands many times. Sir William Farrer, solicitor to Queen Victoria lived there and had a lovely garden and a pond heated by gas so that he could grow exotic plants. Another owner, Lady MacNaughton, employed 17 gardeners. During the Second World War, the property was acquired by the army. It was later saved by Mr. & Mrs. Rudkin and converted into flats. (Mrs. J. Rudkin.)

LST. 4   ACKRILL CORNER LITTLE SANDHURST   Copyright Frith Ltd

83. Acrills corner, named after the family who used to live at this junction of Little Sandhurst High Street, once called Church Road as it lead to St. Michael's Church. This main road going to Wokingham, Ambarrow Farm and the fields are away to the left of the picture. (Mr. C. Sinnott.)

84. Perry Hill House in 1887, from Col. Harvey's album. In July 1884 7 acres of land, bounded by the railway, Church Road, and the footpath, were sold by John Walter to Mary Florence Osborn of Longdown Lodge. She built a house on the site called 'Sunny Rest'. In December 1928 it became the property of Major Hilton-Johnson who changed the name to Perryhill, and so it remains to this day, although there has been housing development in what had been the garden. (Mrs. K. Dancy.)

85. High Street, Little Sandhurst, 1951 must be the printer's code because the postmark says 26th September 1916. (Mr. C. Sinnott.)

Little Sandhurst.

86. Napper's Stores in High Street, Little Sandhurst in 1939, remembered as Napper's Bakery by older residents, a name that makes the taste buds work even to this day. On good Friday morning at about 5am Lily Ceaser and Flo.Grainger used to bring round the hot cross buns made by Harry Ives; special ones for Lady MacNaughton at Sandhurst Lodge because she didn't like candied peel in hers! (Mr. C. Sinnott.)

87. View of Little Sandhurst taken from the Old Scotland Hill School playground. It gives some idea of the climb up to school every morning, and the exuberant race down the hill at the end of the day. The outside lavatories froze in the winter time, and the classrooms had hopeful warmth from the tortoise stoves. (Mr. C. Sinnott.)

88. Old Scotland Hill School. This Wesleyan Methodist School opened for pupils in 1871 to accommodate 140 pupils (mixed). In 1891 reference was made to an average attendance of 72, by 1968 the number on roll was 180 adding the staff headmaster, four full-time assistants and two part-time assistants. With the increase in the population of Little Sandhurst it was decided to build a new school in Grampian Road down in the valley, which is called New Scotland Hill School. The old school was abandoned and eventually pulled down. (Mr. T. Cripps.)

89. The music class at Scotland Hill circa 1910, starting at the back row from left to right: ....,
Adelaide Williams, ..., Joan Hawkins, ..., Alfred Seeby, ..., and William Cornish.
Middle row: ...., Douglas Greenaway ...., ..., Percy Wilkins and Mr. Wilkins. Front
row: ...., ..., ..., ..., ..., ..., Eleanor Sophie Seeby. (Miss V.
Seeby.)

90. This is a Scotland Hill School photo of Group 1, 1927. From left to right, back row: Jack Cox, Ernie Roach, Ted Cripps, Jim Gough, Maurice Birch and Bob Bird. Second row: Bert Le Page, Bob Cashmore, Jos Hayward, Bert Barefoot, John Cashmore, Fred Gough , Reg Bird, Ted Eyles and Mr. Whittle. Third row: Mary Watts, Margery Millard, Mable Hutchins, Eddie Eyles, Flo. Granger, Eddie James, Evelyn Bateman, Hilda James, Len Granger and Frenchy Moth. Front row: Les Bateman, Dorothy Whitehead, Molly Cousins, Emma Green?, Dolly Steel, Rita Norman, Rosy Clarke, Rosy Cox, Jean Hammond and Hilda Hogburn. (Mr. L. Bateman.)

CHURCH ROAD L.SANDHURST.

91. 'Church Road, Little Sandhurst', it says on the card but it is now known as High Street, Little Sandhurst. This view is looking down the undulating road towards Napper's Bakery with Hancombe Road half way down on the right. (Mr. E. Cripps.)

92. Longdown Road, Little Sandhurst. At the Crowthorne Road end of this road was the Temperance Hall now converted into a private house. (Mr. C. Sinnott.)